Our Place in the Universe

Judaism and the Environment

Journal

בַּל תַּשְׁחִית

By
Marc Rosenstein, Tova Sacher, and Sigalit Ur
Galilee Foundation for Value Education

BEHRMAN HOUSE
www.behrmanhouse.com/universe

Much of the material in this book was originally prepared by the authors for internal use at Bialik College, Melbourne, Australia. The authors and publisher are grateful to Bialik College for granting permission to adapt this material for a larger audience.

To the Educator: Please refer to *Our Place in the Universe: Lesson Plan Manual* for complete lesson plans as well as background information, project based learning ideas, puzzle solutions, and more.

Visit www.behrmanhouse.com/universe for links to articles and videos that will deepen your learning about the topics discussed in this book. Encourage learners to explore the free *Our Place in the Universe Game Pack*, filled with fun, content-rich games and puzzles to play online or print out.

Designer: Terry Taylor Studio • Project editor: Dena Neusner • Editorial consultants: Ellen Bernstein, Ellen Rank
Copyright © 2014 Behrman House, Inc., Springfield, New Jersey 07081   www.behrmanhouse.com

ISBN 978-0-87441-912-2 • Printed in the United States of America

The publisher gratefully acknowledges the following sources of photographs and graphic images:
(T=Top, B=Bottom, M=Middle, L=Left, R=Right)
Cover: Shutterstock: SasinT(girl), Incomible(pencil)), Anastacia Zalevska(bike, recycle symbol, tree), MisterElements(bulldozer), topform(star, bulb), Aleks Melnik(scale),artplay(globe, leaf), Phish Photography(10 commandments)9, mexrix(notebook), Ann D. Koffsky(boy)16, Alexey Losevich(boy w/ rabbit), oleschwander(notepaper). Interior: Shutterstock: Jacek Chabraszewsk 2L,22,33BR, Melpomene 2M,31BR, Daisy Daisy 2R,44, GraphEGO 3R,20TM, Alex Staroseltsev 3T,23, mangostock 3BL,20TL, 89studio 3, Antart 5,70, Studio Barcelona 6BL, PHOTOCREO Michal Bednarek 6BR, Triff 7, Eric Isselee 8, Rozilynn Mitchell 10, jorisvo 11, vectorlib.com 12, Leonard Zhukovsky 13TR, S-F 13RM, jejim 13BL, Botand Horvath 13BR, ChameleonsEye 14, Lisa F. Young 15, TaraPatta 17, racorn 18, Tlucadp 18M, Neftali 19B, Inga Nielsen 19T, Africa21, Ortodox 24, vitamin 25BR, Evikka 25B, ledokol.ua 25M, A1design 25T, Eric Isselee 26 BR, Matt Jeppson 26 BL, Morphart Creation 28B, bg: woe 28T, C.M. Corcoran 29 MR, Ales Liska 29 TR, auremar 30T, Risa Towbin Aqua 32T,32B, , Africa Studio 33BL,45B Dariush 34, Catalin Petolea 36T, Hallgerd 36B, Ugo Montaldo 37, Florin Stana 38T, Spirit of America 38B, FWStudio 39, Smit 40T, tassel78 40M, Allies Interactive 40B, 41B, Gaieva Tetiana 41T, You can more 41T, dnaveh 42, night_cat 43B, Sergey Nivens 43T, iralu 45TR, Irene van der Meijs 45TML, garyfox 45114 45 ML, KIM NGUYEN 45 BML, , Jaimie Duplas 46T, MNI 46B, infinity21 47BR, Qpic-Images 47BM, Gelpi JM 48, daulon 50T, Trussel 50B, spirit of America 53BR, Monkey Business Images 54TL, Ditty_about_summer 54TM, Lesya Dolyuk 54BM, MO_SES 54B, Sabphoto 55, Paul Hakimata Photography 56, Marco Prati 57, DNAGraphic John Schwegel 58L, Skrynnik Mariia 58B, kazoka 59T, Laitr Keiows 59M, mexrix 60, smereka 61T, djem 61M, tuulijumala 63BL, martin33 63BR, Gunnar Pippel 64T, dotshock 64B, Butterfly Hunter 65, maxmacs 66, lightpoet 67T, Nata-Art 67B, jannoon028 68, ollirg 69B, Ron and Joe71 BL, Sergey Nivens 72; Wikimedia Commons: GourangaUK 9B, Project Gutenberg 9M, 13TL, Google Art Project 27T, Napoleon Sarony 51, Batni 53BR, US Air Force/Airman 1st Class Nadine Y. Barclay 53BL, Etan J. 52BR, Hans Hillewaert 53TL, Horace Vernet 52BL, Jean-Pol Grandmont 53TR, U.S. Bureau of Reclamation 53ML, user Thande62T, Andreas Praefcke 62B; The 2011 Arava Institute & Hazon Israel Ride 69T.

The Commons Fishing Game adapted from the lesson plan "The Tragedy of the Commons" copyright © by Jeremy Szerlip, Scarsdale, NY.
Excerpt from The Lorax copyright © Dr. Seuss Enterprises, L.P., Random House, 1971.

Library of Congress Cataloging-in-Publication Data
Rosenstein, Marc, 1946-
 Our place in the universe : Judaism and the environment journal / by Marc Rosenstein, Tova Sacher, and Sigalit Ur.
    pages cm
 Includes index.
 ISBN 978-0-87441-912-2
1. Nature--Religious aspects--Judaism--Juvenile literature. 2. Human ecology--Religious aspects--Judaism--Juvenile literature. I. Sacher, Tova. II. Ur, Sigalit. III. Title.
 BM538.N38R67 2014
 296.3'8--dc23
                    2013050288

When God created the first humans, God took them and showed them all the trees of paradise and said: See My works, how beautiful and perfect they are! Everything I have created, I created for you. Take care that you do not spoil and destroy My world, for if you do, there is no one to repair it for you. (*Midrash Kohelet Rabbah* 7:13)

Contents

Authors' Note

Many of the topics discussed in this book are the center of public debate and political conflict, in which scientific questions, morality, cost-benefit analyses, and personal interests can become tangled up. It is important to encourage thoughtful dialogue and to be aware of our own biases. The purpose of the course is not to take a position on vegetarianism, logging, or genetically engineered foods, for instance. The goal is for each of us to think critically about these issues, and to draw on insights from Jewish texts, ideas, and practices as we formulate our own positions.

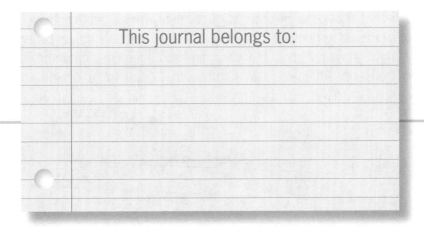

This journal belongs to:

What is our place in the universe?

From the earliest Creation stories to today's news, we humans have been wondering...

- Were we created to rule over the world, and use it for our needs?

- Are we simply a part of nature, like any other animal?

- Do we have a special responsibility for taking care of the world?

Our answers to these questions affect our lives every day, and the lives of future generations. What we eat, how we get around, what we wear: every little decision we make about how we live expresses our belief about our relationship with the world.

In this book you will have the chance to explore the connections between what we believe and how we live. You will discover how Jewish tradition—our values, laws, stories, customs, and sacred texts—can guide us and help us find the right balance.

So, just what is our place, as thinking Jewish human beings, in the universe? Turn the page and let's start our exploration. . . .

Stories We Tell about the World

What is our place in the universe? Does the earth belong to humans, or are we part of it? Are we responsible for taking care of it? There are no easy answers, but the stories that we tell about the world, and about the Creation of the world, can say a lot about our attitudes toward nature. What words come to mind when you think of our relationship as humans to nature, to the world, and even to the universe?

I think our place in the universe is . . .

NATURE AND OUR CREATION STORIES

In the Beginning

The Torah begins with the famous description of the Creation of the world. Open a Bible to Genesis chapter 1, and fill in the day on which each of these was created.

Plants	_____	Light	_____
Fish	_____	Dry land	_____
Stars	_____	Birds	_____
Sky	_____	Cattle	_____
Humans	_____	Sea creatures	_____

Two Creation Stories

Did you know there are actually two stories of Creation in the Torah? Look at Genesis chapter 1, verses 24-31, and Genesis chapter 2, verses 4-19. Notice that the story of Creation seems to start over again in chapter 2, where the history of Creation is retold. Use the chart below to compare the two versions. Make a note of which verses you find the answer in.

	According to Genesis 1	According to Genesis 2
When were humans created—last or first?		
What is humanity's relation to nature?		
Does nature need humans?		

The Genesis Stories and Current Environmental Dilemmas

Choose one of the following environmental dilemmas. Think about it in relation to the two Creation stories in the Torah—Genesis chapter 1 ("fill the earth and master it") and Genesis chapter 2 ("work it and take care of it").

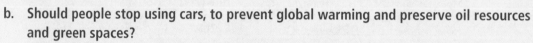

a.   **Should we hunt deer to prevent overpopulation?**
   In many areas of the United States there are calls to reduce deer populations by hunting them, now that their natural predators, like wolves, are mostly gone. When deer populations grow too large, they destroy forests and farms; they are involved in road accidents (about a million each year); they compete with other natural species for food and other resources; and they host the ticks that carry Lyme disease.

b.   **Should people stop using cars, to prevent global warming and preserve oil resources and green spaces?**
   Many scientists claim that people's extensive use of private cars causes global warming, which is changing the climate, flooding coastal areas, and destroying natural habitats. Extensive car use also uses up oil resources and leads to our paving over green areas with highways and parking lots.

<u>Based on Genesis 1, I think</u>

_____
_____
_____
_____
_____
_____
_____
_____
_____
_____
_____
_____
_____

<u>Based on Genesis 2, I think</u>

_____
_____
_____
_____
_____
_____
_____
_____
_____
_____
_____
_____
_____

Humans and the Natural World

The stories from Genesis reflect our understanding of our place in the universe, even if we don't believe that they are historically true. Other cultures may hold completely different views about the relationship between humans and the natural world.

For example, Hindus believe that all animals have souls, and cows are sacred. Jains emphasize nonviolence toward all living creatures, taking extraordinary care not to harm animals. Apaches believe humans and animals are equal partners in the world.

Explain how each culture's belief is reflected in the pictures or story below and on the next page. In what ways are they similar? What can we learn from them?

By the Numbers

1 billion: Number of cars and trucks in the world

35 million: Increase in number of cars and trucks each year

Jainist monks wear masks over their mouths to prevent themselves from accidentally swallowing an insect, and sweep the paths before their feet to avoid stepping on any small animals.

Cows often roam free in India, even along busy streets in cities and towns, like this one in Vrindavan, India. In some states in India where a majority of citizens are Hindu, it is illegal to slaughter a cow.

9

Jicarilla Apache Creation story

In the beginning there was nothing—no earth, no living beings—only the angels.

One day Black Hactcin made the first animal, with four legs and a tail made of clay. So that the animal would not be lonely, he made many other kinds of animals from the body of the first. He sent some to the mountains, some to the deserts, and some to the plains, which is why the animals are found in different places today.

The animals and birds held a council, and they came to Black Hactcin and asked for a companion. Black Hactcin had the animals bring him all sorts of materials from across the land, and he traced an outline on the earth, setting the things that they brought him in the outline. The stones he turned to bones, the sapphire to veins in which flowed ocher turned to blood, the coral became skin, the opal became fingernails and teeth, and the eyes were formed of pearls and jet. Slowly the man rose, until he was standing upright.

Try This! Write, draw, or act out your own original Creation story, which explains the place of humans in the natural world.

THE TOWER OF BABEL: THE PERILS OF PROGRESS

The Tower of Babel

Now the whole world had one language and the same speech. As people moved eastward, they found a valley in Shinar and settled there. The people said to each other, "Come, let's make bricks and bake them thoroughly." They used bricks instead of stone, and tar for mortar. Then they said, "Come, let us build ourselves a city, with a tower that reaches the sky, so that we may make a name for ourselves and not be spread all over the face of the earth."

God came down to see the city and the tower that the people were building. God said, "If when they are all one people speaking the same language they have begun to do this, then nothing they ever plan to do will be impossible for them. Come, let us go down and mix up their speech so they will not understand each other."

So God scattered them all over the earth, and they stopped building the city. That is why the place was called Babel [related to the Hebrew word בָּלַל, "mix up"] because there God mixed up the language of the whole world. From there God scattered the people all over the earth. (Genesis 11:1-9)

How do you think the world would be different if all people spoke the same language?

I think _____

_____

_____

because _____

_____

_____

Try This! With a group, build your own tower. Afterward, think about your group's original goal for the tower.

The Tower of Babel,
Pieter Brueghel the Elder,
1563

Looking for Explanations

What is the point of the Tower of Babel story? Why did God spoil humanity's plan? Here are two commentaries from earlier times:

a. The tower had seven steps in the east and seven steps in the west. They would lift the building stones up from one side and go down on the other side. If a man fell and died, they paid no attention to him. And if a brick fell, they would sit and cry and say, "Woe to us! When will we lift another in its place?" (*Pirkei D'Rabbi Eli'ezer*)

b. They weren't satisfied with the generous gifts of nature that God provided....The people moved from the original natural state of...being happy with their needs being provided for by nature. They wanted man-made things to fill their desires for unnecessary luxuries, and because of this they forgot the true Godly knowledge. (Isaac Abravanel)

I think God stopped the tower from being built because _____

_____

_____

_____

Imagine a modern version of the story, based on the human drive for new and better technologies. Write or draw your story here, or perform it with a friend as a skit or video.

A Modern Babel Story

Puzzle Time: The Tower of Babel Today

Can you match the names to the pictures of these modern day towers? How are these projects similar to or different from the Tower of Babel? Go to www.behrmanhouse.com/universe to check your answers and find out some interesting facts about each of these buildings.

A.

B.

1. Burj Khalifa (Khalifa Tower) Dubai, United Arab Emirates

2. European Parliament Buildings, Strasbourg, France

C.

3. Sydney Opera House, Sydney, Australia

4. One World Trade Center (Freedom Tower), New York City

5. Three Gorges Dam, Yangtze River, China

D.

E.

Nature in Jewish Laws and Customs

What do Jewish traditions have to do with the environment? Judaism is not only based on the stories we tell, but on the behaviors we are expected to do. This chapter presents several examples of Jewish values and traditions that teach us how to behave toward nature. Write your own rules for how we should treat nature:

1. Remember to

2. Take time to

3. Be careful not to

4. Be kind to

5. Don't forget that

We celebrate nature in the sukkah during the Jewish harvest holiday of Sukkot.

B'RACHOT: RECEIVING NATURE'S GIFTS

What Is a B'rachah?

What words or images come to mind when you think of the word *b'rachah*, "blessing"? Write or draw them in the diagram, then write a definition below.

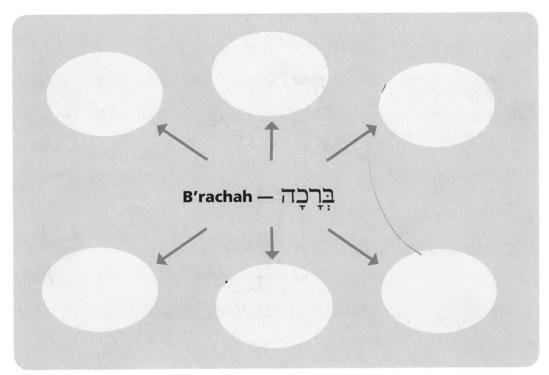

B'rachah — בְּרָכָה

A b'rachah or blessing is _____

_____

_____

_____

_____

_____

_____

Can you say the *b'rachah* for each of these items?

Me and My B'rachot

We experience the world with our whole body. Draw lines from the experiences listed to the appropriate parts of the body. Then match the *b'rachot* (blessings) to the occasions or situations in which they are said, by writing the corresponding letter in the space provided.

A. When you see lightning or high mountains or great rivers or any unusual natural phenomena

B. When you see fruit trees flowering in the spring

C. When you eat bread

D. When you drink water or soft drinks

E. When you hear thunder

F. When you smell pleasant spices, plants, or flowers

G. When you put on new clothes

____ Praised are You, Adonai our God, Ruler of the world, who creates all types of perfumes.

____ Praised are You, Adonai our God, Ruler of the world, who didn't leave anything out of God's world and created good things and good trees so people may enjoy them.

____ Praised are You, Adonai our God, Ruler of the world, who has given us life, sustained us, and enabled us to reach this time.

____ Praised are You, Adonai our God, Ruler of the world, who brings forth bread from the earth.

____ Praised are You, Adonai our God, Ruler of the world, whose strength and power fill the world.

____ Praised are You, Adonai our God, Ruler of the world, who does acts of creation.

____ Praised are You, Adonai our God, Ruler of the world, that all was created by God's word.

What can saying blessings and other expressions of gratitude teach us about our place in the world?

_____

_____

Compose a Blessing

Think of a moment you have experienced in nature when it would have felt good to say a blessing of wonder and appreciation. Close your eyes and imagine that moment again. Then draw the experience, find a photograph of it, or describe it in words.

Now compose a blessing for that moment. You can start with the traditional words or with any words you like.

_____

_____

_____

_____

_____

_____

_____

_____

_____

BAL TASHCHIT (DO NOT DESTROY)

Everyday Impact

Some activities are clearly harmful to the environment. But what about our everyday activities? Think of a common, everyday activity (like eating a meal, watching TV, or being driven to school). Draw or attach a picture of it here:

How does this activity impact the environment? Check all that apply, or fill in your own description of its environmental impact.

☐ Creates garbage that will fill landfills

☐ Pollutes the air

☐ Makes noise, creating noise pollution

☐ Uses natural resources

☐ Uses electricity (generation of electricity often creates air pollution)

☐ Requires the use of objects that were manufactured using electricity

☐ Has an engine that uses gasoline or another fossil fuel (a fuel that pollutes the air and that can't be replaced)

☐ Requires transportation of people or objects by a vehicle that uses fossil fuels

☐ _____

☐ _____

☐ _____

☐ _____

By the Numbers

450: Gallons of water used to make a quarter-pound hamburger (to grow the grain for the cow to eat, to process the meat, to grow the tomatoes for the ketchup, etc.)

2.75 million: Miles of paved roads in the United States.

Bal Tashchit

Open a Bible to Deuteronomy 20:19-20, and fill in the blanks:

The Torah says that you may destroy trees that _____,

but you may *not* destroy _____ trees.

Why do you think the Torah makes this distinction?

_____

_____

The principle we have seen in the Torah was later extended very widely to prohibit any kind of unnecessary destruction, and was referred to as *bal tashchit, (*בַּל תַּשְׁחִית*)*, "do not destroy." Here's how Maimonides explains it:

> This does not refer to trees alone, but also to he who breaks dishes, and tears clothes, and demolishes a building, and blocks a spring, and destroys food: he is sinning against *bal tashchit*.
> (Maimonides, Laws of Kings chapter 6, 14)

What do all the examples given by Maimonides have in common?

_____

_____

Some kinds of destruction may be justified, such as tearing down a building that has become dangerously unstable. Choose one of the items listed in the quote by Maimonides, and give an example of something that might be a good reason for destroying it.

_____

_____

Maimonides

Moses Maimonides was a famous Jewish rabbi, doctor, and philosopher who lived in Egypt in the twelfth century. His summary of Jewish law *(Mishneh Torah)* and his book of philosophy *(Guide For the Perplexed)* are two of the biggest Jewish best sellers of the past 800 years.

What's Your *Bal Tashchit* Score?

Answer the following questions, counting your points as you go.
When you're done, see how much impact you have on the environment.

1. **How do you get to school?**
    a) On foot or riding a bike (1 point)
    b) School bus or carpool (2 points)
    c) In a car alone (3 points)

2. **What do you eat?**
    a) Vegan or vegetarian diet (1 point)
    b) Occasionally eat meat (2 points)
    c) Eat meat every day (3 points)

3. **What kinds of snacks do you choose?**
    a) Mostly fresh fruits and vegetables, nuts (1 point)
    b   A mix of fresh foods and processed foods with a lot of packaging (2 points)
    c) Mostly processed, packaged snack foods (3 points)

4. **How many of the following materials do you discard regularly, without recycling?**
    (choose all that apply)
    a) Paper (1 point)
    b) Plastic (1 point)
    c) Cardboard (1 point)
    d) Glass (1 point)
    e) Electronic devices (1 point)
    f) Food waste (1 point)

How did you score?

3-5 points: Maimonides would be proud of you!

6-9 points: Pretty good, but try to learn how you can be more nature friendly.

10 or more points: Look for ways to reduce your impact on the environment.

Can you add more questions to this quiz? (Note that you will have to change the scoring totals if more points can be accumulated.) Quiz your friends and family, too!

Question 5: _____

_____

_____

a) _____ (1 point)

b) _____ (2 points)

c) _____ (3 points)

Question 6: _____

_____

_____

a) _____ (1 point)

b) _____ (2 points)

c) _____ (3 points)

Try This! Think of one change you can make in your life right now to lower your *Bal Tashchit* score… and do it.

TAKING A BREAK: SHABBAT AND SH'MITAH

What Is Not Ours

Imagine that a good friend leaves for camp and lets you borrow his expensive racing bike. You are free to use it while he's away if you take care of it, as long as you don't shift into the highest gear. He explains that the gearshift is sensitive and the speed can be dangerous, and he doesn't want any harm to come to the bike—or to you. You are out riding with a friend one day and come to a huge, smooth, empty parking lot with a slight slope. Your friend challenges you to a race. You lose. "You know," he says, "if you'd shift into high gear, you'd go faster. Let's race again...."

What would you do?

I would _____

_____

_____

because _____

_____

_____

How should we treat things that don't belong to us? Is the world ours to do with it as we wish?

_____

_____

_____

_____

_____

_____

Rest and Renewal

Remember Shabbat and keep it holy. Six days shall you labor and do all your work, but the seventh day is a Sabbath of Adonai your God: you shall not do any work—you, your son or daughter, your male or female slave, or your cattle, or the stranger who is within your settlements. For in six days Adonai made heaven and earth and sea, all that is in them, and rested on the seventh day; therefore Adonai blessed the Sabbath day and made it holy. (Exodus 20:8-11)

According to this commandment, number four of the Ten Commandments, why are we supposed to rest on Shabbat?

_____

_____

How can we—and our world—benefit from a day of rest? Use as many of these words as you can in your answers:

☐ borrowed   ☐ rest   ☐ limit

☐ use up   ☐ families   ☐ renew

☐ resources   ☐ spiritual   ☐ world

_____

_____

_____

The Roman philosopher Seneca couldn't understand the idea of Shabbat. He wrote:

The Jews waste away a seventh of their lives by putting in one day (of rest) in seven days...

Write an answer to Seneca, based on the environmental benefits of Shabbat.

Dear Seneca,

The Sabbatical Year

Among the rules that Moses gave the children of Israel as they were getting ready to enter the Promised Land was this:

> For six years you shall sow your fields and for six years you shall prune your vines and you shall gather in their produce. And in the seventh year there shall be a Sabbath of complete rest for the land, a Sabbath for the Lord; you shall not sow your field, and you shall not prune your vineyard....But you may eat whatever the land during its Sabbath will produce [on its own]...The land is Mine; you are merely strangers whom I allow to live on My land. (Leviticus 25:3-4, 6, 23)

This law is called *sh'mitah*, (שְׁמִיטָה) the Sabbatical year. What would be the challenges of obeying *sh'mitah*? What might be some practical solutions?

_____

_____

_____

How is *sh'mitah* similar to or different from Shabbat?

Sh'mitah		Shabbat
	How hard/easy is it to observe	
	Benefits for people	
	Benefits for the land/world	
	What we learn from it	

Did You Know?
Recent and upcoming Sabbatical years in Israel are: 5768 (2007-8), 5775 (2014-15), and 5782 (2021-22). The Sabbatical year always begins on Rosh Hashanah.

See if you can find all these sevens in the Jewish calendar and tradition..

Across

2. The seventh letter of the Hebrew alphabet (not counting "vet")
5. The biblical ruler who dreamed a dream of sevens
7. The seventh year, when the land rests
9. The second king of Israel, who had seven older brothers
10. A unit of time made up of seven days
11. What God did on the seventh day
12. What was created on the seventh day

Down

1. The holiday that falls on the first day of the seventh month and marks the New Year
3. The seventh month in the Hebrew calendar
4. The holiday that falls seven weeks after Passover and celebrates the giving of the Torah
6. The Hebrew name for the spring holiday that lasts seven days
7. The seventh day, a day of rest
8. A ritual object with seven branches

The Animal Kingdom

How should we treat animals? Should our needs take priority over theirs? Just as there are rules for how we should treat fellow humans, Judaism (like other religions) gives us guidelines for how we should treat our fellow animals and how we should balance our needs with theirs. What do you think?

Animals are valuable to the world because _____

_____

_____

We should treat animals with _____

_____

_____

_____

because _____

_____

_____

Sometimes this is difficult because _____

_____

_____

On the path, draw two more pairs of animals that you think should also be in the ark.

Noah's Ark, Edward Hicks, 1846

BIODIVERSITY

Noah's Ark

Read about Noah and the ark in Genesis 6:9-22. Which of the following animals do you see in the painting? Mark a ✓ beside them. Mark an ✗ beside the animals that are missing from the painting.

☐ snakes   ☐ horses   ☐ rats   ☐ goats

☐ spiders   ☐ zebras   ☐ sheep   ☐ skunks

I think the artist chose these animals and left out others because

_____

_____

_____

Why did God tell Noah to save *all* animals, even the insects? Here's one explanation:

> God explicitly mentioned the creeping things of the ground because he knew Noah might think that God didn't mean to include the insects, for they are unnecessary, and he should not bother himself to save them, for the world would be better off without them. That is why God mentioned them—for even though their usefulness is hidden from Noah, it is not hidden from God. (Rabbi Isaac Karo)

I think the world would/would not (circle one) be better off if Noah had not saved

the insects, because _____

_____

_____

_____

27

King David and the Spider

Are all species potentially useful to humans? This story from Jewish tradition provides one way of thinking about the question. Read the story, and then act it out.

Narrator: One day, long before he became king, the young David was sitting in his garden when he saw a wasp eating a spider.

David: God, what good are these creatures? The wasp just eats the honey, and the spider spins all year but produces no cloth.

God: David, don't look down on my creatures; there will come a time when you will need them.

Narrator: Soon after, King Saul thought that David was rebelling against him. The king chased David, who hid in a cave. God sent a spider that spun a web across the opening of the cave.

King Saul: Look, no one has entered here, for the spider's web is not torn. Let's go search for David somewhere else.

Narrator: When David emerged from the cave and saw the spider, he sang the praises of the Master of the Universe.

David: God, who can tell of Your great deeds, for *all* Your creations are good.
(from *The Alphabet of Ben Sira*)

Can you think of examples of species that may be useful to us, even if we don't yet know how?

Bio•di•ver•si•ty (noun) is the variety of different species of plants and animals in an environment. Which kind of environment—tropical rainforests, other forests, grasslands, deserts, oceans—do you think has the highest biodiversity? Which has the lowest biodiversity?

Did You Know?
The dodo was a large, flightless bird from the island of Mauritius that became extinct in the seventeenth century. It drew attention to the extinction of species due to human activity and was immortalized in *Alice's Adventures in Wonderland*.

The Case of the Spotted Owl

Spotted owls live in the forests of the Pacific Northwest. In the 1980s, conservation groups became worried that so many trees were being cut down for lumber that it was endangering the owls by destroying their habitat. Environmentalists petitioned to ban logging activity in the area in order to preserve this rare species. Logging companies responded that a logging ban would mean that thousands of workers would lose their jobs, causing massive poverty in the region.

Have a class debate: **Should logging be banned in the forests of the Pacific Northwest to protect the spotted owl from extinction?**

1. Search online for more information. (You can follow the links on www.behrmanhouse.com/universe.)

2. With a partner, choose one group to represent (circle one):
   - Environmentalists
   - Logging company owners and leaders
   - People who work for logging companies
   - Hikers in Pacific Northwest forests
   - People who live near Pacific Northwest forests

By the Numbers

37: The number of species of mammals that are endangered, threatened with extinction in the United States

3. Prepare your arguments.

Yes, logging should be banned because . . .	No, logging should not be banned, because . . .

4. Take turns presenting your arguments to the rest of the class. Try to reach an agreement.

Resolution: _____

TZA'AR BA'ALEI CHAYIM
(KINDNESS TO ANIMALS)

Animals and Us

We share the world with lots of nonhuman animals, large and small, wild and tame. Do they care about us? Should we care about them?

Here are some ways I interact with animals:

Wild animals: _____

Farm animals: _____

Pets: _____

Other: _____

_____

There is often tension between the needs of humans and the needs of animals. From the Torah, we learn the mitzvah of *tza'ar ba'alei chayim* (צַעַר בַּעֲלֵי-חַיִּים), avoiding cruelty and showing kindness to animals. This principle can help us understand how to balance human and animal needs.

Taking Care of Animals

Imagine that your class was going to adopt a class cat. List all the things you can think of that the cat would need, as well as your class's needs.

The cat needs . . .	We need . . .

How hard is it to balance these needs?_____

_____

_____

What the Torah Tells Us: Humans and Animals

Read the texts below, which describe *mitzvot*, commandments, about how to treat animals. Draw lines to match each of the texts on the left to the lessons we can learn on the right. The same lesson can apply to more than one rule, and each rule can teach us several lessons.

Texts	Lessons
1. If you see the donkey of someone who hates you fallen under its load, you must not ignore him, but be sure to help him with it. (Exodus 23:5)	A. Don't stand by when you see animals suffering.
2. A person cannot sit down to eat until he has fed his animals. (Babylonian Talmud, *B'rachot* page 40A)	B. Take care of your animals before you take care of yourself.
3. If you happen to notice a bird's nest along the road, whether in a tree or on the ground, and there are chicks or eggs with the mother bird sitting on them, you must not take the mother with the young. You must be sure to let the mother go, but you may take the young for yourself. (Deuteronomy 22:6-7)	C. Appreciate and repay the help animals give you by helping them.
	D. You are responsible to take care of your animal's needs.
4. You must not muzzle your ox when it is threshing grain. (Deuteronomy 25:4)	E. Don't upset animals unnecessarily.
5. When an ox, lamb, or goat is born, it must be under the care of its mother seven days, but from the eighth day onward it will be acceptable as an offering gift to the Lord. You must not slaughter an ox or a sheep and its young on the same day. (Leviticus 22:27-28)	F. Treat animals compassionately.
	G. We can use animals for our own needs.

Rewrite one of the ancient texts above for our world today:

_____

_____

_____

_____

_____

_____

Should We Eat Animals?

In the Torah, right after the Creation of the world, God tells Adam and Eve what they are allowed to eat:

> I now give you every seed-bearing plant on the face of the entire earth and every tree that has fruit with seed in it. They will be yours for food. And to all the animals of the earth, and to every bird of the air, and to all the creatures that move on the ground—everything that has the breath of life in it—I give every green plant for food. (Genesis 1:29-30)

We may eat:

We must not eat:

After the flood God repeats these instructions to Noah, but with a difference:

> You may eat any moving thing that lives. As I gave you the green plants, I now give you everything. But you must not eat meat with its life (that is, its blood) in it. (Genesis 9:3-4)

We may eat:

We must not eat:

Why do you think the rules changed?

_____

_____

_____

_____

_____

_____

Moderation

How often do you eat meat? Check one.

Every day	Several times a week	Once a week	Occasionally	Never

What are some reasons for or against eating meat, for yourself and for the world?

Health: _____

_____

Environment: _____

_____

Animals' suffering: _____

_____

Taste: _____

_____

Cost or availability: _____

_____

Here's what Maimonides says about eating meat:

> A person should only eat meat when he has an appetite for it....and it's enough for a healthy person to eat meat only once a week. If he's wealthy enough to eat meat every day, he may.
> (*Mishneh Torah*, Laws of Opinions 5:10)

As we have seen, there are many factors to consider in finding the right balance between our needs and the needs of other creatures. Eating meat doesn't have to be an all-or-nothing decision—perhaps the answer lies in moderation, rethinking how much meat we eat.

Try This! Collect meat-free recipes from friends and family members and make a vegetarian class cookbook.

Below is a list of biblical verses. Every verse in this list mentions an animal or animals that lived in Israel in biblical times. Look up the verses in a Bible to identify the animals, then complete the crossword puzzle.

Across

5. Amos 3:8
6. Job 39:13
8. Deuteronomy 32:11
10. Genesis 49:27
12. Genesis 8:7
13. I Kings 5:6

Down

1. Judges 15:4
2. Genesis 8:8
3. Psalms 104:17
4. Jonah 2:1
7. Job 39:26
9. Job 39:1
11. Genesis 49:21

Write your thoughts about how we use or take care of animals.

Sharing Public Resources

Who does nature belong to? If nature belongs to no one, then who is responsible for taking care of it? And if it belongs to everyone, then can everyone use it? Are there limits? The question of who owns land, air, water, and other shared resources of the world is a difficult one and has led to plenty of wars over the centuries. In this chapter we'll look at how Jewish thinkers have approached this dilemma.

I think natural resources belong to

_____

_____

_____

You are responsible for taking care of natural resources if you

_____

_____

_____

The natural resources I use every day are

_____

_____

_____

THE COMMONS

Our Shared Resources

How many natural resources can you think of that are shared, used, and enjoyed by all?

_____

_____

_____

These shared resources are often referred to as "the commons," because they belong to everyone in common but not to anyone in particular.

The Commons Fishing Game

The interests of the individual and the group can easily come into conflict over shared resources. To see how, play this fishing game. Visit www.behrmanhouse.com/universe for directions. Track the fish statistics of your group using the following chart:

	Number of fish in the lake (after reproduction)	Number of fish caught per year by your family	Total number of fish caught per year
YEAR 1			
YEAR 2			
YEAR 3			
YEAR 4			
YEAR 5			
TOTAL			

What happened in the game? Did players take more fish than they needed? Why or why not? What happened to the population of fish in the lake?

Did You Know?
The population of bluefin tuna in the Atlantic Ocean has declined 70 percent in the last 30 years due to overfishing. They may soon become extinct.

Stone Pollution

The concept of "the commons" is discussed in the Talmud, such as in this story.

One must not remove stones from one's own land into the commons. Once there was a farmer who removed stones from his field onto the road. A wise man came upon him and said: "Fool! Why are you moving stones from land that isn't yours to land that is yours?" The farmer laughed at the wise man.

After a time, the farmer had to sell his field. He no longer owned the land.

Then one day he was walking on the road and stumbled upon the stones he had thrown there. He said: "That wise man knew what he was saying when he asked me why I was removing stones from land that wasn't mine to land that was…"

(Babylonian Talmud, *Bava Kama* 50b)

Write and illustrate your own version of this story in the comic strip panels below. Use an example from the modern world in place of the farmer and the stones (such as a factory and pollution), to illustrate the idea of the commons.

Once there was...	After a time...	Then one day...

Workers cleaning up an oil spill from a tanker, Huntington Beach, California, 1990

USING WATER WISELY

We Need Water For...

List all the ways you and your family use water.

_____   _____

_____   _____

_____   _____

Why Do We Need Rain?

Open your Bible to Deuteronomy 11:10-12 and read the passage about the importance of rain in the land of Israel. Then fill in the blanks, using the words in the word bank below:

In Egypt, the _____ provided water for their _____ from

the Nile River, through their own hard work. But the land in Israel gets its water from

_____ . Farmers there are _____ on nature and God to provide

water. This should teach us that water is _____ and precious, and we should

use it _____.

Word Bank

dependent

farmers

limited

fields

sparingly

rain

Did You Know?
In Israel the rainy season lasts from October to April. In the summer months, no rain falls at all.

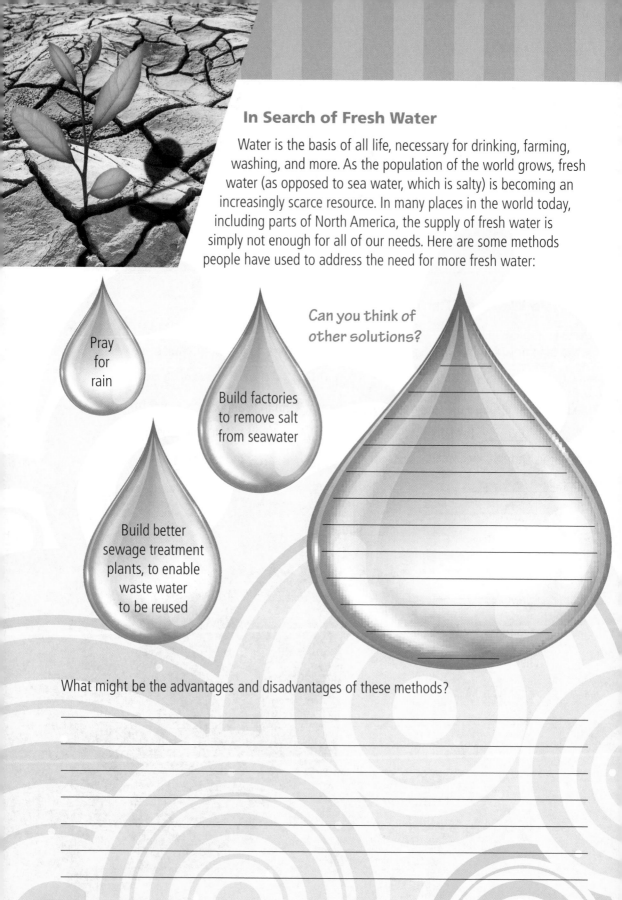

In Search of Fresh Water

Water is the basis of all life, necessary for drinking, farming, washing, and more. As the population of the world grows, fresh water (as opposed to sea water, which is salty) is becoming an increasingly scarce resource. In many places in the world today, including parts of North America, the supply of fresh water is simply not enough for all of our needs. Here are some methods people have used to address the need for more fresh water:

Pray for rain

Build factories to remove salt from seawater

Build better sewage treatment plants, to enable waste water to be reused

Can you think of other solutions?

What might be the advantages and disadvantages of these methods?

How Can I Conserve Water?

One of the best solutions for addressing our need for more water is to reduce how much we use. Write or draw three suggestions for saving water in each part of the house.

Bathroom

_____
_____
_____
_____
_____
_____
_____

Kitchen

_____
_____
_____
_____
_____
_____

Yard

_____
_____
_____
_____
_____
_____
_____

Laundry Room

_____
_____
_____
_____
_____
_____

Visit www.behrmanhouse.com/universe for links to water-saving ideas that you can do at home.

Prayer for Rain

In ancient times, droughts were seen as a sign of punishment from God. It was believed that only by mending our ways and praying to God could we hope to cause rain to fall at the appropriate time. Below are excerpts from the prayer for rain that is said in some synagogues on Shemini Atzeret, at the end of Sukkot. Read it responsively as a class.

Our God and God of our ancestors:
Remember Abraham, who was drawn behind You like water. You blessed him like a tree planted alongside streams of water. You shielded him, You rescued him from fire and from water. You tested him when he sowed upon all waters.
> *For his sake, do not withhold water!*

Remember Jacob, who carried his staff and crossed the Jordan's water. He dedicated his heart and rolled a stone off the mouth of a well of water. He wrestled with an angel made of fire and water. Therefore You pledged to remain with him through fire and water.
> *For his sake, do not withhold water!*

Remember Moses, who was drawn forth in a bulrush basket from the water. He drew water and provided the sheep with water. At the time Your treasured people thirsted for water, he struck the rock and out came water.
> *For his sake, do not withhold water!*
> *For the sake of their righteousness, grant abundant water!*

For You are our God, Who makes the wind blow and makes the rain fall.
> *For blessing and not for curse. Amen.*
> *For life and not for death. Amen.*
> *For plenty and not for scarcity. Amen.*

The Jordan River in the north of Israel

Write your own prayer for rain and water conservation.

_____

_____

_____

_____

_____

_____

_____

_____

_____

_____

_____

_____

_____

_____

_____

_____

_____

_____

Our Responsibility to the Future

How do our choices today affect the people of tomorrow? The Torah frequently mentions the importance of passing down our stories and traditions to future generations. We don't just live for ourselves, but we are expected to care about those who will come after us. This applies to how we treat nature and its resources, as well. Will we use them up or preserve them for the benefit of people who will live long after we are gone?

Some of nature's resources that I use are

I need or want to use these resources because

But if I use them up, then

We should care about future generations, because

HOW MUCH IS TOO MUCH?

The Waste Inventory

Often we go about our lives without really stopping to think about what we use and what we waste. Try this project, as food for thought: For three days, take a few minutes several times each day to fill in this chart.

	Day 1	Day 2	Day 3
Edible food that I threw away today			
Other stuff that I threw away today			
On any of the days, take a look around your room for items to list below.			
Items I own but never use (clothes, tools, toys, etc.)			

I could reduce the amount I waste by

_____

_____

_____

_____

_____

_____

What is the harm in wasting things, or buying and using more than we need?
Check off the answers you agree with, and add your own explanations:

☐ Producing extra stuff uses up more natural resources.

☐ Transporting more products uses more energy.

☐ Larger amounts of trash cause more pollution.

☐ _____

☐ _____

☐ _____

☐ _____

☐ _____

☐ _____

Did You Know?
About a trillion plastic bags, weighing four million tons, are produced in the world in a year. Ninety percent are thrown away. The plastic bags we throw out today will remain in landfills for hundreds of years before they decompose.

A Waste-Free Ideal

The rabbis of the Talmud noticed that the date palm tree is 100 percent useful:

> Look at the date palm tree, of which nothing goes to waste: the fruits are eaten, the fronds are used for the lulav on Sukkot, the branches are used for shade, the fibers are made into rope, the twigs are woven into sieves, and the trunk is used for roof beams. (*Midrash B'reishit Rabbah* 41:1)

Sketch an example of another plant or animal that is or could be 100 percent useful to humans, with no part thrown away. Label the various uses:

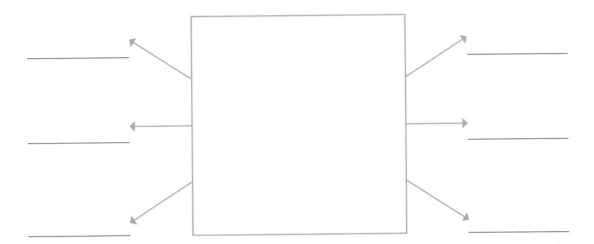

Take another look at your Waste Inventory on page 45. Can you make use of some of the things you discarded, instead of throwing them out?

I could reuse _____ *to do* _____

_____

I could give _____ *to* _____

_____

I could reuse _____ *by making it into* _____

_____

_____

_____

How Much Is Enough?

The Talmud asks, "Who is a rich man?" It then goes on to suggest several answers:

1. "He who is content with his wealth," says Rabbi Meir.

2. Rabbi Tarfon says: "He who has a hundred vineyards and a hundred fields and a hundred slaves to work them."

3. Rabbi Yossi says: "He whose toilet is close to his table." (In those days, most people did not have an in-house toilet unless they were very wealthy.) (Babylonian Talmud, Shabbat 25b)

I most agree with _____

because _____

_____

_____

_____

According to this definition, I have enough stuff if _____

_____

_____

_____

Write your own answer to the question, "Who is rich?"

Someone who _____

_____

_____

_____

_____

_____

_____

_____

_____

The Tenth Commandment

"You shall not covet your neighbor's house . . . or his servants, ox, or donkey, or anything that belongs to your neighbor." (Exodus 20:14)

The word *covet* means _____

_____

_____

Sometimes it's hard not to covet things, because _____

_____

_____

Advertising, peer pressure, and other factors encourage us to consume, or use, more than we need. Sometimes we confuse the difference between what we want and what we need. List examples of things you own in each category.

Things I need	Things I want

How many things in the "need" column do you *really* need? Circle them. Is it okay to buy things just because you want them? Why? How much is too much?

_____

_____

_____

_____

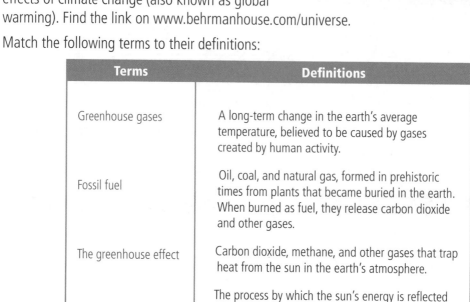

CLIMATE CHANGE

What Is Climate Change?

Watch the National Geographic video *Global Warming 101*, which explains the causes and effects of climate change (also known as global warming). Find the link on www.behrmanhouse.com/universe.

Match the following terms to their definitions:

Terms	Definitions
Greenhouse gases	A long-term change in the earth's average temperature, believed to be caused by gases created by human activity.
Fossil fuel	Oil, coal, and natural gas, formed in prehistoric times from plants that became buried in the earth. When burned as fuel, they release carbon dioxide and other gases.
The greenhouse effect	Carbon dioxide, methane, and other gases that trap heat from the sun in the earth's atmosphere.
Climate change	The process by which the sun's energy is reflected back to Earth by gases in the atmosphere, so it can't escape, and warms the Earth.

I think climate change might/might not (circle one) affect my life because

_____

_____

_____

_____

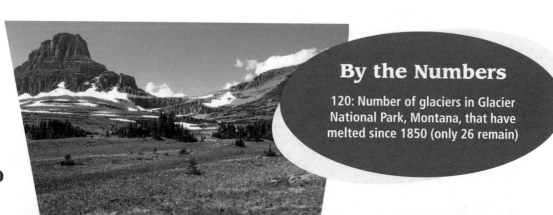

By the Numbers

120: Number of glaciers in Glacier National Park, Montana, that have melted since 1850 (only 26 remain)

Choni Sleeps for Seventy Years

Climate change is a long-term process, one that requires us to think about future generations. Even at the time of the Talmud, the rabbis were concerned about planning for the future, as the following story shows.

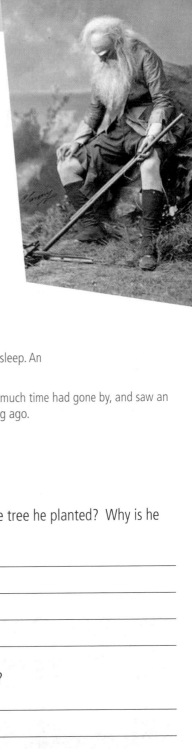

> One day, a wise man named Choni was walking along and saw an old man planting a carob tree. Choni inquired, "How long does it take for a carob tree to bear fruit?"
>
> The man replied, "Seventy years."
>
> Choni asked, "Are you sure you will live for another seventy years to enjoy the fruits of your labor?"
>
> The man explained, "I came into a world full of grown carob trees. Just as my ancestors planted those trees for me, so, too, I plant for my descendants."
>
> Choni continued on his way, until he sat by the roadside to rest and fell asleep. An outcropping of rock hid him from sight and Choni slept undisturbed.
>
> Seventy years passed, and finally Choni awoke. He rose, unaware of how much time had gone by, and saw an old man picking fruit from the carob tree that he had seen planted so long ago.
>
> Asked Choni, "Are you the man who planted this tree?"
>
> The man replied, "No, I am his grandson."
>
> (Adapted from the Babylonian Talmud, *Ta'anit* 23a)

Does the old man know the people who will eat the fruits of the tree he planted? Why is he working for their benefit?

_____

_____

_____

_____

What can this story teach us about the issue of climate change?

_____

_____

_____

_____

_____

Renewable Energy

We use energy to turn on our lights and computers, to run our cars and trains, and to power our factories and machines. Much of our energy is made from fossil fuels, which have formed over eons and are not renewable. In addition, these fuels produce greenhouse gases that contribute to climate change.

The good news is that people have been using renewable energy sources since ancient times, and modern technologies can harness the power of the sun, wind, water, and geothermal heat (heat generated by the earth's interior).

See if you can match the pictures to the descriptions of how they generate energy.

1. WATER pressure is used to generate electricity.

2. South-facing windows help the SUN warm the building.

3. WIND power is used to grind grain for flour.

4. The earth's HEAT is used in natural hot springs to cook or bathe.

5. Underground HEAT generates electricity.

6. The energy of the SUN is harnessed by solar panels.

7. WIND over the sea generates power.

8. WATER power is used to grind grain for flour.

B) Windows in a church in Spain

A) Windmill in an eighteenth-century French painting

C) Windmills off the Belgian coast

E) Twelfth-century water mill in Germany

D) Grand Coulee Dam, Washington State

F) Ancient Roman bath fueled by a hot spring

G) Solar power plant in Nevada

H) Geothermal power plant in California

LARGE TASKS, SMALL STEPS

Who, Me? Causes of Climate Change

Here are pictures of some common activities. In what ways do you think they contribute to global warming?

Watching TV

_____
_____
_____
_____

Riding in a car

_____
_____
_____
_____

Eating a hamburger

_____
_____
_____
_____

Flying in an airplane

_____
_____
_____
_____

Draw another common activity.

_____
_____
_____
_____

Small Steps

Have you ever been confronted with a task that looked so big that you gave up on it even before starting it? How did that make you feel?

☐ Disappointed   ☐ Hopeless   ☐ _____

☐ Discouraged   ☐ Overwhelmed   ☐ _____

☐ Unhappy   ☐ Anxious   ☐ _____

Write a poem or a paragraph about the experience, or write a letter giving advice to someone facing a similarly hard challenge.

_____

_____

_____

_____

_____

_____

_____

Saving the world from climate change is a huge task, and it's tempting to think that we have no chance of succeeding, so why should we try? A story about Rabbi Akiva may be encouraging:

> Rabbi Akiva, at the age of 40, had not begun to study Torah and assumed it was too late to even begin to master it. But one day he noticed the stone at the lip of the well had been eroded to make a channel for the water. He asked who had cut the rock and was told it had been cut by the water, drop by drop. He concluded that if water could cut rock, little by little, then he could learn Torah, word by word and line by line. He began to study and became a great scholar. (*Avot D'Rabbi Natan*)

From this story, we can learn that _____

_____

_____

_____

_____

_____

_____

Tikun Olam

Jewish tradition teaches us the mitzvah of *tikun olam*, (תִּקּוּן עוֹלָם), which means "repairing the world." This idea is especially important now, when it seems that human activity may be "breaking" the world. List ten things we all can do to reduce global warming, then create a poster to display your ideas to others in your school or community.

1. _____
2. _____
3. _____
4. _____
5. _____
6. _____
7. _____
8. _____
9. _____
10. _____

Now take that first step. Choose one item and commit to carrying it out this week.

This week I will _____

_____

_____

Next week I will _____

_____

_____

Try This! How big is your carbon footprint (the amount of greenhouse gases produced by your daily activities)? Visit www.behrmanhouse.com/universe for a link to a carbon footprint calculator, and find out.

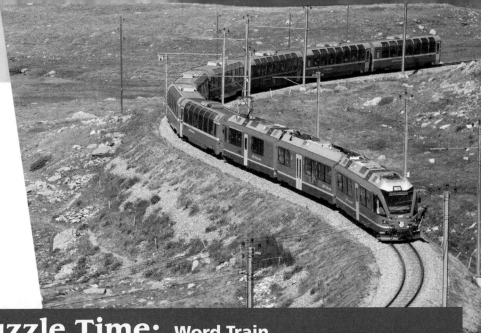

Puzzle Time: Word Train

Below is a list of things you can do to reduce your carbon footprint, the amount of greenhouse gases produced by your daily activities. Fill in the blanks in the sentences below, then fit the answers into the puzzle. The answers form a train: each word begins with the last letter of the previous word.

1. A long-life _____ lights up your room with less electricity than a standard bulb.

2. Walk or ride a public _____ to school instead of going in a car.

3. Taking a _____ is better than taking a bath, as it uses less hot water and takes less energy to heat the water.

4. Use _____ batteries instead of disposable ones.

5. Turn off _____ appliances when you're not using them.

6. Learn how to transform leftover food and garden waste into _____ , to reduce the amount of garbage that needs to be transported .

7. Plant a _____; it will take in carbon dioxide and breathe out oxygen.

57

Setting Limits

What if you could change the way things work in the world, in the name of progress? It would be hard to resist. It's part of our nature as human beings to be curious, to investigate the world, and to use our learning to try to improve nature for our own benefit. We've developed amazing technologies in the field of medicine, as well as in more controversial fields like genetic engineering and nuclear energy, that involve changes to the very way things work in nature. But are there limits? Or are we free to make such changes, especially if they have clear benefits to humanity?

If we could change the laws of nature, I would _____

_____

_____

_____

_____

_____

_____

_____

There should/should not (circle one) be limits because _____

_____

_____

_____

_____

_____

_____

GENETIC ENGINEERING: ARE WE PLAYING GOD?

Creating New Life Forms

Since humans began to care for animals and cultivate plants they have engaged in crossbreeding, by finding an organism with useful characteristics and crossing it with one with different characteristics. Over the years we have created new varieties that meet our needs, like roses without thorns, disease-resistant cucumbers, or cows that thrive in hot weather. Normally such crossbreeding can only be done within the same species; one of the few exceptions is the mule, which is a cross between a horse and a donkey.

Imagine all the new combinations you could make if you could crossbreed different species. Perhaps you could help solve food or water shortages, or reduce pollution or global warming. For example: cross corn with cactus to get a food crop that can grow in a dry desert; or cross a horse with an ox to provide a fast, powerful animal for farm work in developing countries.

Create and draw your idea for a new animal or plant here. Include notes to explain how this new species would benefit people or the world.

Must We Leave Nature Alone?

Even if we can cross species, should we? Here are two views from Jewish sources:

1. And God made the beasts of the earth according to their species, and the cattle according to their species, and everything that creeps upon the ground according to their species; and God saw that it was good. (Genesis 1:25)

   The reason that we are forbidden by the Torah to mix species is that God created the species and gave them the ability to reproduce, so that each species would exist forever. And God commanded that this should be unchanging, which is why the Torah says "according to their species." (Rabbi Moses ben Nachman, also known as Nachmanides)

Explain Nachmanides's commentary in your own words.

_____

_____

_____

2. Once Rabbi Ishmael and Rabbi Akiva met a sick man. They gave him instructions for what to do to be cured.

   He asked them, "Who made me sick?"

   They answered, "God."

   He said, "You have interfered in matters that are none of your business—God made me sick and you try to heal? Aren't you going against God's will?"

   So they said to him, "What is your profession?"

   "I am a farmer."

   "Who created the vineyard?"

   "God."

They said, "You are interfering in matters that are none of your business—God created it, but you harvest the fruit."

He said, "But if I didn't plow and mulch and fertilize and weed, nothing would grow."

They said, "Just as the tree, if it is not cultivated and fertilized and watered, will die, so it is with our bodies." (from _Otzar Hamidrashim_)

Explain this story in your own words.

_____

_____

What does Jewish tradition teach us about our freedom to intervene in nature?

_____

_____

Genetic Engineering

Today, scientists can take a gene from one organism and insert it in another, without crossbreeding. This is called genetic engineering, and it can have real benefits. For example, scientists can transfer a gene into corn from a bacterium that is resistant to a certain weed killer. With this new corn, farmers will no longer have to plow up weeds; they can simply spray the whole field with weed killer, and all the weeds will die, but the corn will be fine.

Below are some possible effects of this new corn. Sort the effects into Pros and Cons by writing a brief summary of each effect into the appropriate column in the chart. Then circle the effect that seems most important to you. Should there be rules limiting genetically modified crops? Who should be making these decisions?

Effects of genetically modified corn	
PRO	CON

1. Can save millions of people from hunger by creating more productive crops, able to grow under harsh conditions.

2. Can greatly reduce farmers' use of nonrenewable fuels made from coal, oil, and gas.

3. New weeds might develop that are resistant to weed killers, which could be harmful to agriculture in the long run.

4. We don't know what other effects there might be, such as negative health effects from eating lots of genetically modified corn.

5. Other possible effects: _____

_____

_____

NUCLEAR ENERGY: EVALUATING RISKS

The Golem of Prague

This well-known Jewish legend about sixteenth-century Prague, where Jews were being persecuted, addresses the difficulty of balancing benefit and risk.

In the city of Prague, there lived a learned and pious man named Rabbi Judah Loew. One night, the rabbi heard a voice in a dream telling him, "Make a creature of earth to save your people!" Troubled, the rabbi looked through his books to find the meaning of the dream. In one of the most ancient books in his library, he discovered instructions to make a golem.

The rabbi enlisted two of his disciples and went with them to the banks of the river. There they made a creature of mud and clay. Rabbi Loew circled the creature seven times, reciting the words he had read in his book, and then wrote the Hebrew word אֱמֶת (*emet*, truth) on the golem's forehead. Lo and behold, the creature rose up and bowed before the men. Rabbi Loew told the golem, "You have been created to help and protect the Jews of Prague!"

That night, the rabbi's wife turned to him, troubled, and asked, "Is it not a sin to make a living creature?"

"It has no life but that which the Sacred Name gave it," replied the rabbi.

"I am afraid," said the rabbi's wife, but he paid her no heed.

In the following weeks, the rabbi put the golem to good use. He protected Jewish children when they were bullied by their neighbors, he broke up a fight between two angry men, and he even rebuilt the run-down section of the synagogue. Every Friday afternoon, the rabbi would rub out the first letter from the word on the golem's forehead, changing the word אֱמֶת (*emet*, truth) to מֵת (*met*, dead), and so the golem was laid to rest for the Sabbath.

One Friday the rabbi was so busy that he forgot about the golem. As he joined the community in welcoming Shabbat in the great Altneuschul [Old-New Synagogue], he heard a commotion in the street. He rushed outside and saw the golem tearing through the streets, breaking windows, setting fire to houses, tossing people aside. Rabbi Loew went to meet the raging golem, holding out his hand in command. The golem hesitated, faltering, and the rabbi erased the letter from his forehead. The rabbi looked at the golem's lifeless body sprawled at his feet, gazed around the ruins of the town, and said, "No more! Carry him up to the attic!"

From that day onward, the Jewish community of Prague made do without its golem, and legend has it that his broken remains still lie in the attic of the Altneuschul.

Try This! Imagine that you could create a creature like the golem that could do anything. Would you create such a creature? Why or why not? What would you command it to do? Write a comic strip or create an animation about the creature.

The Altneuschul in Prague, the oldest active synagogue in Europe, completed in 1270

What Is Nuclear Energy?

The story of the golem can be seen as a metaphor for nuclear energy. Nuclear power holds great promise—it's a clean, renewable energy source, emitting minimal pollution and requiring only small amounts of natural resources. It also holds great risks.

In the twentieth century, physicists discovered that certain atoms are unstable and could be split, releasing energy that could be used to heat water and generate electricity. At the same time, some of the energy makes other atoms unstable, in a chain reaction. The energy created is clean and doesn't use up limited natural resources, unlike more traditional energy sources like oil, natural gas, and coal. However, if this chain gets out of control, it can create way too much heat and even an explosion (as in an atomic bomb). The challenge is to keep it under control and to safely get rid of all the dangerous, unstable waste atoms that are generated along the way.

What do you think are the benefits and dangers of using nuclear energy?

Using Nuclear Energy	
Benefits	**Dangers**

What rules should there be governing the operation of nuclear power plants?
Who should be making these decisions?

Visit www.behrmanhouse.com/universe for more information
on the risks and benefits of nuclear energy.

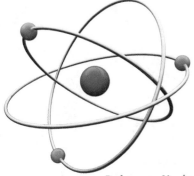

Dukovany Nuclear Power
Station, Czech Republic

Striking the Right Balance

How can we find the right balance between what is good for humans and what is good for nature and for the world? Sometimes we make poor decisions, even when we have good intentions. But we can make a difference in *tikun olam*, "repairing the world," both on a personal level and on a national or global scale. In this chapter, we'll look at some exciting new developments in Israel and North America, and we will create a set of guidelines for preserving the environment. At the heart of it all is the central question: What is our place in the universe?

I think our place in the universe is _____
_____
_____
_____
_____

Take a look at your response to this question at the beginning of chapter 1, on page 6. Has your response changed? Why or why not?

_____
_____
_____
_____

THE HULA VALLEY: THE LAW OF UNINTENDED CONSEQUENCES

A Flock of Birds

Once upon a time there was a kingdom that was overrun by flocks of birds, and its people worried that the birds would eat all the wheat in the fields and there would be famine in the land. The king issued a decree that every person in the kingdom had to bring a certain number of birds to the court to be killed. Whoever did not fulfill this duty would be fined one gold crown. The king's purpose was to kill the birds before the wheat sprouted and grew.

The king's decree reached some areas before the wheat grew, and the people obeyed the king's command and killed the birds. Immediately there were worms in the roots of the wheat stalks, which sucked the very core of the wheat. The wheat rotted away, and there was famine in the land. But in the areas that did not receive the king's decree, the people left the birds alone, and the birds ate the worms. The wheat survived, and the crops were plentiful.

(*Me'am Lo'ez* on *Pirkei Avot* 3:2)

The law of unintended consequences states that our actions in a complicated situation may create unexpected and unwanted results. How is this story an example of this principle? Have you ever done something that had unintended consequences?

What I did was _____

_____

_____

_____

What happened next was _____

_____

_____

_____

I didn't expect this to happen because _____

_____

_____

_____

Draining the Hula

Watch the beginning of the Jewish National Fund movie describing the draining of the swamps in Israel's Hula valley. You can find the link at www.behrmanhouse.com/universe. Think about whether the project was a success, as described in the film. Jot down any notes or questions here, as you're watching.

_____

_____

_____

_____

_____

And the Results?

Choose a topic: water quality, bird migration, animal species, or soil quality. Sort through the Consequence Cards (which can be printed from www.behrmanhouse.com/universe) to find the three cards for your topic.

Describe in your own words the consequences of the Hula valley drainage project on your chosen topic.

_____

_____

_____

_____

_____

Did You Know?
In the 1990s, part of the Hula valley was reflooded, creating a haven for tens of thousands of migrating birds.

Unintended Consequences Revisited

See if you can predict the consequences of the following human interventions around the world. How easy or hard is it to do? (Circle one or more results for each event.)

Event	How did this affect the environment?
1. A hunter introduced 24 wild rabbits to his property in Australia in 1859 for hunting purposes.	a. Some local animals became extinct. b. The soil eroded. c. The number of wolves in Australia increased.
2. For more than a century, North Korea has been clearing many of its forests to make land available for agriculture.	a. Bird migration patterns changed. b. Electricity production was damaged. c. Millions of people starved to death.
3. Large numbers of fish are caught each year from lakes in Africa.	a. More people fall ill. b. Lake water temperature rises. c. Lakeside sheep are smaller.

Now check your answers below.

> When God created the first humans, God took them and showed them all the trees of paradise and said: "See My works, how beautiful and perfect they are! Everything I have created, I created for you. Take care that you do not spoil and destroy My world, for if you do, there is no one to repair it for you."
>
> (Midrash Kohelet Rabbah 7:13)

Answers:

1. a and b—The rabbits multiplied and ate so much that some local animals died out for lack of food. In addition, the rabbits ate so many plants that the soil eroded because there were no plant roots to hold it down.

2. b and c—With no trees to hold soil in place, it washed into power plants and halted production. Rainwater flowed faster on cleared land, flooding fields, ruining the crops, and causing massive starvation.

3. a—Fish eat the snails that transfer the disease schistosomiasis; when there are fewer fish, there are more snails and more disease.

INNOVATION AND INSPIRATION

The Lorax's Message

Watch the trailer for the movie *Dr. Seuss' The Lorax*. (Find a link to it at www.behrmanhouse. com/universe.) The movie is based on a Dr. Seuss book about a man, the Once-ler, who comes to a beautiful place and starts cutting down Truffula trees to make a product called a thneed. He builds bigger and bigger factories to make more and more thneeds, all the while polluting the area and driving the wildlife away, despite the Lorax's warnings. Finally he cuts down the last tree and all that is left is a wasteland.

In the book, after all the Truffula trees have been cut down and the Lorax and all the animals have left, the Once-ler turns to the reader and says:

UNLESS someone like you cares a whole awful lot

Nothing is going to get better. It's not.

He drops the last Truffula seed, and continues:

You're in charge of the last of the Truffula Seeds.

And Truffula Trees are what everyone needs.

Plant a new Truffula. Treat it with care.

Give it clean water. And feed it fresh air.

Grow a forest. Protect it from axes that hack.

Then the Lorax and all of his friends

may come back.

(from The Lorax, by Dr. Seuss.)

Write a list of five things that you could have done to prevent the pollution and damage caused by the Once-ler's uncontrolled production of thneeds.

If I were there, I would . . .

1. _____

2. _____

3. _____

4. _____

5. _____

Environmental Initiatives

Jews around the world are creating new ways to help the environment. For example . . .

Touring Israel on the Hazon Israel Ride

Hazon, from the word *chazon,* which means "vision" in Hebrew, is an important Jewish environmental organization.

Look up different programs that Hazon offers on its website: www.hazon.org/programs.

Which one would you be most interested in joining? Why? _____

_____

_____

_____

_____

Kibbutz Sde Eliyahu is an eco-friendly kibbutz in northern Israel. Look up the environmentally friendly products and techniques that the kibbutz produces and uses, through the link on www.behrmanhouse.com/universe. Choose one, and design an advertisement or commercial for the product or technique. Be sure to indicate the problem being addressed, and how the solution promotes development while preserving resources.

Sketch your ideas below and then create a poster or a skit and present it to the class.

Product name: _____

Controlling the population of fruit flies

Rabbi Tarfon taught: "It is not your responsibility to finish the work but you are also not free to avoid it." *(Pirkei Avot 2:21)*

69

FROM KNOWLEDGE TO ACTION

Where Do We Go from Here?

KNOWLEDGE: Write at least three new things you learned
in this course, including stories, information, ideas, and concepts.

I learned

_____

_____

_____

_____

I found out

_____

_____

_____

_____

I realized

_____

_____

_____

_____

ACTION: In the Talmud, our sages teach, "Study is greater than action, because it leads to action." (*Kiddushin* 40b) Write any changes you have made in your behavior as a result of something you learned in this course.

I used to

_____

_____

_____

_____

But now I

_____

_____

_____

_____

Ten Commandments for the Environment

In small groups, brainstorm a new set of commandments for helping to preserve the environment. First, individually write down your ideas for environmental commandments on Post-it Notes. Then gather the related ideas together, and, as a group, decide on the 10 most important commandments. Write them below, or make a poster to share with the class.

Ten Commandments for the Environment

1. _____

2. _____

3. _____

4. _____

5. _____

6. _____

7. _____

8. _____

9. _____

10. _____

I, _____,
[your name here]

hereby pledge to do my best to keep the

Ten Commandments for the Environment

today and every day.

_____
(signature)

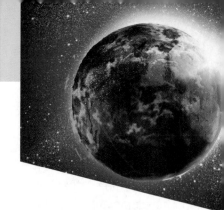

WORDS TO KNOW

Bal Tashchit
The biblical principle that discourages unnecessary destruction; literally, "Do not destroy." (p. 19)

Biodiversity
The variety of different species of plants and animals in an environment. (p. 28)

B'rachah/B'rachot
A blessing; an expression of gratitude, wonder, or appreciation in response to an experience. (p. 15)

Carbon Footprint
The amount of greenhouse gasses produced by daily activities. (p. 56)

Climate Change
A long-term change in the earth's average temperature, believed to be caused by gases created by human activity; also known as global warming. (p. 50)

Commons, The
Resources that are shared, used, and enjoyed by all. (p. 37)

Endangered Species
A species that is present in very small numbers and is in danger of dying out. (p. 29)

Extinction
The situation that results when a species has died out and ceases to exist. (p. 29)

Fossil Fuels
Oil, coal, and natural gas, formed in prehistoric times from plants that became buried in the earth and are today burned as fuel. (p. 50)

Genetic Engineering
The process of taking a gene from one organism and inserting it into another. (p. 61)

Law of Unintended Consequences
The idea that our actions in a complicated situation may create unexpected and unwanted results. (p. 65)

Nuclear Energy
A renewable energy source created from the splitting of atoms. (p. 63)

Renewable Energy
Power that is taken from resources that are continually replenished, such as sun, wind, and water. (p. 52)